FRUIT OF THE SPIRIT

JOY

Fruit of the Spirit Study Guide Series

Love

Joy

Peace

Patience

Kindness

Goodness

Faithfulness

Gentleness

Self-Control

CALVIN MILLER

 FRUIT OF THE SPIRIT

JOY

Published in Nashville, Tennessee, by Thomas Nelson. Thomas Nelson is a trademark of Thomas Nelson, Inc.

Thomas Nelson, Inc., titles may be purchased in bulk for educational, business, fund-raising, or sales promotional use. For information, please e-mail SpecialMarkets@ThomasNelson.com.

Typesetting by Gregory C. Benoit Publishing, Old Mystic, CT

ISBN: 978-1-4185-2840-9

Printed in the United States of America

11 12 QG 7 6 5 4

TABLE OF CONTENTS

But the fruit of the Spirit is love, joy, peace, patience, kindness, goodness, faithfulness, gentleness and self-control. Against such things there is no law.

—Galatians 5:22–23

INTRODUCTION

There is a difference between joy and happiness. Joy is the emotional response to God's presence in our lives; happiness is the emotional response to our circumstances in life. Joy is internal; happiness is circumstantial. Joy remembers salvation and anticipates eternity long before it caves in to today's pressures.

Like the other fruits of the spirit, joy is an aspect of God's being. God doesn't become joyful; he is joyful. Therefore, as we grant him more and more control over our lives, his characteristic of joy will overwhelm our tendencies to be angry, self-centered, and frustrated.

In our lives, we can easily allow Satan to rob us of our joy by turning our attention to our circumstances rather than to our relationship with God. It is a struggle to keep our focus on God. We must continually refocus our attention.

There is little in this world that can bring us lasting joy. We might have moments of elation, but joy as a way of life is rare even among those who consider themselves to be followers of Christ. We all want to be joyful but we can't seem to find the source.

That's where God comes in. In this study, we will see that joy is something that comes into our lives when we ask Jesus into our hearts. God knew that joy would be elusive, therefore he made it available through his Spirit.

We are brought to the point of joy when we view a sunrise over the eastern horizon and when we hold a newborn baby for the first time. We experience joy when we hear children playing and laughing because the cares of this world have yet to rob them of their innocent joy. We experience joy when we witness a new believer step forward in an expression of faith. Joy is in the creation. Joy is in the Creator.

As we make this journey together, look for opportunities to let God renew your joy. In the end, people will be drawn to God because they see his characteristic of joy in your life.

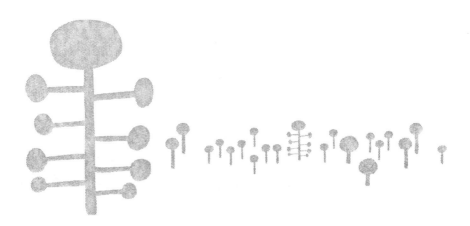

HOW TO USE THIS GUIDE

Galatians 5:22–23 is not a plan to achieve better faith. Rather, it is a description of God's personal gifts to all of us. If we follow God and seek his blessing, then the fruits of the Spirit are a natural overflow in our relationship with God. We are to grow in character so that one day we will reflect the image of our Lord.

This series of nine six-week studies will clearly focus your spiritual life to become more like Christ. Each study guide is divided into six weeks, and each of the six-week courses covers one of the fruits of the Spirit. Participants simply read each daily study and answer the questions at the end of each devotional. This prepares everyone for the group discussion at the end of the week.

Each week features a similar pattern that explores one aspect of that study's fruit of the Spirit. The first lesson establishes the aspect of the fruit to be explored throughout the week. The second lesson looks at the week's theme as it relates to God's purpose in the life of the believer. The third lesson looks at the week's theme as it relates to the believer's relationship with Christ. The fourth lesson explores how the fruit is relevant in service to others. And in the fifth lesson, the theme is related to personal worship. A sixth lesson is included as a bonus study, and focuses on either a biblical character who modeled this particular fruit, or a key parable that brings the theme into focus.

Each weeklong study should conclude in a group review. The weekly group discussion serves as a place to understand the practical side of the theme and receive encouragement and feedback on the journey to become more Christlike. For the study to have the character-transforming effect God desires, it is important for the participant to spend ten to twenty minutes a day reading the Scripture passage and the devotional, and to think through the two questions for the day. If each participant reads all of the questions beforehand, it greatly enhances the group dynamic. Each participant should choose three or four questions to discuss during the group session.

These simple guidelines will help make group time productive. Take a total of about forty-five minutes to answer and discuss the questions. Each person need not answer every question, but be sure all members participate. You can stimulate participation by having everyone respond to an icebreaker question. Have each group member answer the first of the six questions listed at the end of the week, and leave the remaining questions open-ended. Or, make up your own icebreaker question, such as: What color best represents the day you are having? What is your favorite movie? Or, how old were you when you had your first kiss?

No one should respond to all of the questions. Keep in mind that if you are always talking, the others are not. It is essential that everyone contribute. If you notice that someone is not participating, ask that group member which question is the most relevant. Be sensitive if something is keeping that member from contributing. Don't ask someone to read or pray aloud unless you know that the member is comfortable with such a task.

Always start and end your time with prayer. Sometimes it helps to have each person say what he or she plans to do with the lesson that week. Remember to reserve ten minutes for group prayer. You might want to keep a list of requests and answers to prayer at the back of this book.

Week 1: The Joy of Creation

Memory Passage for the Week: Psalm 19:1–2

Day 1: The Joy of Creation

Joy cannot survey the marvels of God's creation and keep silent. Genesis 1:1–5.

Day 2: The Purpose of God in My Life

God's Word reveals many truths that have the sole purpose of restoring joy to the discouraged. Job 38:1–7.

Day 3: My Relationship with Christ

When we come to Christ in prayer, whatever gloom we carry seems to transform into joy and hope. Matthew 6:28–30.

Day 4: My Service to Others

Our service to others should be offered with a smile from deep inside our souls. Unless we offer joy with every crust of bread, our offerings fall short. James 2:14–17.

Day 5: My Personal Worship

In God's presence we can't help but find joy and exhilaration. Psalm 19:1–4.

Day 6: A Character Study on Miriam

Exodus 15:21

Day 7: Group Discussion

Day 1: The Joy of Creation
Read Genesis 1:1–5

In the first week of the world's existence, God created the heavens and the earth. And on the first day of that week—there in the middle of dark chaos—God created light. What a wonder! Light! Splitting dead nothingness like a laser instrument, driving malignant darkness from the universe. Light! Traveling at 186,000 miles per second at the very command of God—light! Bringing things that could not be seen to eyes as yet uncreated. God breathed the words *fiat lux* ("let there be light") and smiled at this instantaneous phenomenon of both science and grace. God smiled because he knew that the power of his glorious first light would in time make vision possible.

God saw the light and smiled, for it was good. Was this God celebrating his own ego?

Let us never accuse God of arrogance. Jehovah has no ego that needs self-congratulation. He does remark that what he created is good, but he does not create light that he may brag about it. After all, to whom would he brag? He created light so his stars could talk to each other across great distances. He created light so a cold world could orbit a distant sun and find its silver track warm enough for life. He created light so that lasers, supernovas, and galaxies could all proclaim themselves. He created light to warm and illuminate all things cold and dark.

But light isn't merely a physical energy form. Light is spiritual. God created light because darkness is hopeless stuff. He created light so that despair will have no place to hide. When God said, "Let there be light," the angels must have broken into glad *hallelujahs*. For when light comes, the natural response of all who behold it is joy. Joy cannot survey the marvels of God's creation and keep silent. The angels must have been hushed by the sight of the beauty of all God had created. But those angels, at first awed by all he made, surely found their next response to be joy.

Questions for Personal Reflection

1. Does God's creation bring you joy?

2. What do you love most that God has created?

Day 2: The Purpose of God in My Life

Read Job 38:1–7

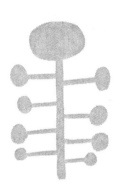

Come rejoice and offer God this prayer:

God, when I contemplate creation, I know you are God. When I face your godhood, I remember why I am in the world. It is your godhood that puts me in my place. I must face the same questions you asked Job: Where was I when you laid the foundations of the world? Where was I when you stretched out the heavens like a canvas? Where was I when all the morning stars sang together?

Humbled by the immensity of your creation, I must ask these questions. I am hushed by its beauty. I am stopped by its size. Before your vast existence, I am forced to remember that I am small, atom-like, and of little consequence in the scheme of universal things. Yet you saw me, and even as you did with Job, you began a conversation with me. And as we talked I saw you in the natural world, and I sang anthems to your great creativity. I sang things like, "Morning has broken" and "How marvelous are your works."

And after I had praised you for your creative works, I knew that whatever purpose you had in my life should be my single reason to live. For you made me just as you made my world. And my joy gives birth to gratitude that you included me in your beautiful world.

God, I know your purposes in my life are most important. And when I see the works of your hands, I know you want my hands to create also. I'm here to use my body—fearfully and wonderfully made—to create life warm and usable. So give me the gift of transforming the cold chains of heartache into the bright, new kingdom of

God. I want to touch hate and rename it love. I want to touch vengeance and rename it mercy. I want to touch resentment and rename it understanding. I want to touch defiance and rename it submission. Create in me a servant who worships you and cherishes the kingdom Jesus died to establish, amen.

Questions for Personal Reflection

1. Have you discovered God's purpose for your life?

2. Does knowing God's purpose bring you joy to share?

Day 3: My Relationship with Christ
Read Matthew 6:28–30

When Jesus wanted to teach his disciples the art of depending on his sufficiency, he invited them to consider the lilies of the field. Here the exquisite fashioning of God fell on the most common of wildflowers. Jesus used God's little flowers as evidence that God could be trusted to take care of all of our needs—great or small.

The result of Christ's all-sufficiency is joy. We can look at the greatness of his river-chiseled canyons and feel joy welling up within us. But we can also look at the finesse of a field flower and feel the same rush of glory. The same God who overwhelms us with the ocean can mystify us with a drop of clear, pure dew shaken from the petals of a rosebud.

To encounter either his wide grandeur or his tiny gem-like creations is to awaken his anthem in our soul. Joy is our response to the creation of God. And it is his Son, Christ, who awakes us to the fullness of his wonder. It is the Jesus of the wildflowers who calls us to marvel at the lilies, and when we have seen his perfect creation we know we can depend on him.

Let us never forget that Jesus was an outdoors man. His entire ministry was a three-year campout with his disciples. We find him more often living outside than inside. His miracles of calming the storm, walking on the water, or feeding the five thousand are all outdoor miracles.

In such rapport with the elements and all of nature, it is natural that Christ's sermon illustrations have to do with rain, harvest, and wildflowers. Here's to our fairest Lord Jesus. Here's to the Jesus of the wildflowers. Let us go to the lilies and praise him.

Questions for Personal Reflection

1. Do you see ways in which God has provided for your needs, whether small or great?

2. Where do you see joy in God's creation?

Day 4: My Service to Others
Read James 2:14–17

Joy is the uncontainable expression of our faith. But joy is not something God gives us just so we can experience a spiritual high. Joy is meant to be the consistent response of our lives. We have been investigating the joy that results from seeing the creativity of God, but God also wants to use our lives to create a better world for those around us. So joy comes from our willing service to others.

When we see someone in need of ministry, and we know we could do something to help, but fail to follow through, the experience of joy is lost. The fullest joy is ours when we know we are used by God to create a better life for needy souls that God puts in our path.

We were created to be God's crown of nature. It is natural for us to get hungry and thirsty, to grow tired and cold. To celebrate our humanity fully we must seek not only to take care of our own needs, but to care in the same way for the needs of others. This is our ministry to the world—to care and care genuinely.

God creates life—our lives and the lives of those needy souls he calls us to serve. But the joy that belongs to us cannot come until we learn to serve all God has created and offer them a better quality of life. Then we will have taken time to care. Only then will we have earned an honest joy. Caring and healing as Jesus himself did is the shortest path to joy. Such service reminds us that we are partners with God in extending his kingdom by blessing his hurting world with our own commitment to Christ.

Questions for Personal Reflection

1. Have you ever seen someone who needed help and failed to help them? How did you feel?

2. How do you help others to have a better quality of life?

Day 5: My Personal Worship
Read Psalm 19:1–4

In this psalm, nature is honored with flamboyant praise. If ever your joy grows weak, take your Bible to a lonely hillside, study the Scriptures, and open your life to praise where the horizon is wide, the air is fragrant, and the clouds tend toward silver. In such a place, it is impossible to keep your joy to yourself.

The ancient Egyptians and Greeks often looked to the skies and there, etched in the fiery distant stars, they drew pictures of their gods and goddesses, their demons, dragons, and heroes. But the psalmist looked up to the stars and saw that beneath the entire canopy of space there was only one great constellation. This constellation, etched by all the stars at once, formed a picture of God.

The heavens declared the glory!

The skies preached!

Further, the heavens and skies could not be silenced. The beauty of the cosmos awoke the dull earth with its singing spirit. Do not command the cosmos to be silent. God is in love with beauty. Nature is in love with its Creator. It will not be silent—ever! Always it will praise him.

When God finished each day of creation in Genesis, he remarked that "it was good." We are close to God when we stop and appreciate all that he created. When we stop and survey all that he has made, we can only exalt his work and cry, "It is good!"

So may it be with your soul. May your joy set your lips alive with praise and inflame your heart with love. May the beautiful things of God never permit you a speechless moment. Rather, get loud before his glory and praise him with unending joy.

Questions for Personal Reflection

1. Do you remember to stay in God's presence and let him fill you with joy?

2. Do you thank him for the joy he brings?

Day 6: Miriam—The Voice of Praise
Read Exodus 15:21

Praise is our reflexive response to joy. When we meet God, we feel elation. When we are elated, we must praise.

Miriam is a complex character. She is first mentioned in Exodus 2:1–8,
where she watched her mother put the infant Moses in a little basket
and float him through the marshes of the Nile. Miriam was responsible
for watching over the floating baby—her little brother—until Pharaoh's
daughter discovered him. It was then that Miriam forthrightly suggested,
"Shall I go and get one of the Hebrew women to nurse the baby for you?"
(Exodus 2:7). Pharaoh's daughter agreed, and Miriam arranged for Moses'
own mother to be the nursemaid.

In this commendable deed, Miriam appeared kind and compassion-
ate. But later we also learn that Miriam could be critical. She, along with
Aaron, criticized Moses for taking a Cushite (or Ethiopian) wife. This
wife was probably not Zipporah, who was a Midianite (v. 21); multiple
wives were common, especially among sheiks and leaders, and Moses
was definitely a leader. Why Miriam criticized Moses for this is not clear.
However, Miriam was afflicted with leprosy for the criticism.

Still, Miriam is most remembered for the spontaneous siege of joy
that gripped her life after the Egyptian army was buried in the Red Sea.
Praise is glorious, and blessed are those who can seize a moment, see
God in that victorious moment, and break into spontaneous praise.

Israel had been delivered. In many ways crossing the Red Sea in the Old Testament is the equivalent of the cross and resurrection in the New Testament. They both stand for victory, and both are miracles of redemption. Israel would forever celebrate this crossing as the time when God saved them. Later Christians would celebrate the cross and resurrection as the time when Christ saved them. But if Israel would make this the center of their highest praise for centuries yet unborn, it was Miriam who saw it at the time.

God had acted! God had saved!

History had been made! A nation had been forged!

Miriam's joy was authentic and her praise very real as she sang:

> *Sing to the LORD,*
> > *for he is highly exalted.*
> *The horse and its rider*
> > *he has hurled into the sea.*
> —Exodus 15:21

Questions for Personal Reflection

1. Are you elated to be in God's presence?

2. Do you seize every opportunity to praise God for filling you with joy?

Day 7: Group Discussion

The following questions should take about forty-five minutes to answer and discuss. Each member should answer the first question, leaving the remaining questions open-ended. Everyone need not answer, but be sure all members participate.

1. *Where is the most beautiful place (outdoors) you have ever been?*

2. *What do you do to appreciate the beauty of the world around you? Do you ever thank God for his beautiful world?*

3.   *When you look around and observe God's creation, how does it make you feel?*

4.   *Have you ever experienced the joy that comes from caring for someone in need?*

5. *When you experience joy, do you ever express that joy in praise?*

6. *What is one thing from this study that you want to remember and apply to your life?*

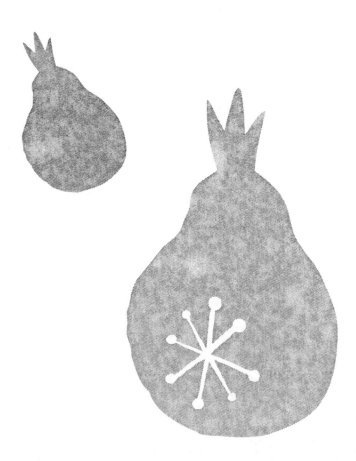

Week 2: Joy and Praise

Memory Passage for the Week: 1 Thessalonians 5:16

Day 1: Joy and Praise

When joy is missing, we are captive to the *blahs*. But the outcome of praise is always joy. 2 Samuel 6:14–15.

Day 2: The Purpose of God in My Life

The existence of a day-to-day positive attitude will produce joy, and this joy will accompany a person wherever he or she goes in life. Ecclesiastes 8:14–15.

Day 3: My Relationship with Christ

If we praise God—even when we don't feel like it—we will soon find ourselves praising God because we *do* feel like it. Psalm 30:4–5.

Day 4: My Service to Others

The book of Isaiah suggests that drawing large numbers to God may depend on our developing a sense of authentic praise. Isaiah 42:1, 10–13.

Day 5: My Personal Worship

When we behold the supernatural power of God, we are at first hushed and then set afire with outbursts of joy and praise. Leviticus 9:22–24.

Day 6: A Character Study on David

Psalm 23

Day 7: Group Discussion

Day 1: Joy and Praise

Read 2 Samuel 6:14–15

There is a progression in the various steps of joy. We begin to enter into joy with feelings of warmth that heighten to euphoria, then swell to elation, and may —as in the case of this passage—end in rapture and dance.

Almost every world religion has a sect within it that focuses on spiritual ecstasy or joy, including Christianity. The outcome of praise in every denomination is always joy. We all love the effervescence of our praise because it produces this joy. When such joy is missing, we are captive to the *blahs*. The blahs are the result of pressing on with life when the joy we wish we hadn't lost is gone. At such moments we can understand why David cried in Psalm 51:12: "Restore to me the joy of your salvation."

David brought the ark of the covenant into Jerusalem. It was his desire that this chief artifact of Israel's sojourn in Sinai be in the royal city. Why? Because the Jews believed that God himself dwelt on the *kapporeth*—the lid of the ark. Wherever the ark was, there was the dwelling place of God. David brought the ark into his new capital because he wanted God near him as he directed the nation. Furthermore, if God was near him, then his praise would center on the nearness of God, and his joy would be continual and vibrant.

Once we savor spiritual joy, we will never be happy until we taste it yet again. Happy are those who attend a worship service and find that those who lead in worship put them in touch with a holy God. Worship leaders who understand this know that when they have done their best work, they have performed the miracle of bringing God near.

Questions for Personal Reflection

1. What is missing in your life?

2. What will it take to make you happy?

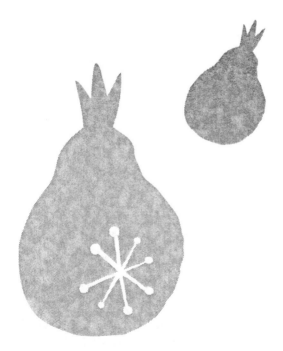

Day 2: The Purpose of God in My Life

Read Ecclesiastes 8:14–15

The writer of Ecclesiastes is convinced that the best short-term solution for unhappiness in life is to get up every morning, put on a happy face, and convince yourself you're going to enjoy life. Some positivists speak of the importance of a "be happy" attitude. If this seems too intentional, let the writer of Ecclesiastes convince us that the best way to be happy in life is to be intentional about it.

This passage seems to suggest that moods do not track us down and force themselves upon us. Our moods should not be the master of our circumstances. We should be master of both our circumstances and our moods.

Happiness is a choice, and misery is an option. When we agree with God that we are going to be joyous by intention, we are pretty much saying that happiness will not be left to circumstances or to other people. Generally, when our joy is missing we tend to blame one or the other. But for any set of circumstances or any people to make us unhappy, we do, in a sense, have to agree to it. God wants us to consistently choose the joy option as our way of life. That is the message of this very short and intentional verse in Ecclesiastes.

"But," some might object, "isn't joy a by-product of our relationship with God? Shouldn't we try to get our relationship right, and the joy will come automatically?" No doubt this is one way to achieve joy, but a corollary truth is that we should be able to simply obey this directive from

Scripture. We should do this whether we feel like it or not. Whatever our mood, we should assume an attitude of joy. Deliberately choosing this as our way of life, the mood in which we approach our days will manifest joy. So Ecclesiastes reinforces our hope of the positive life by simply commanding us to take charge of our moods and choose joy.

Questions for Personal Reflection

1. Do you believe happiness is a choice?

2. How do you try and maintain a positive attitude?

Day 3: My Relationship with Christ

Read Psalm 30:4–5

Perhaps the place to begin our Bible study is to ask this question: "When the word *Jesus* comes to your mind, does a smile dominate your consciousness?" Your relationship with Christ should be such a pleasant affair that merely to think of his name tends to kick your emotional deportment up a notch or two.

Jesus brings joy. It is his name that sponsors our best joy.

A few years back I was traveling on an airplane, and as I sat, I watched a flight attendant as she served her none-too-gracious public. She never seemed to run into any emotional snags. She was sparkling—so effervescent, it was hard not to be impressed with her joy. Finally, I took a chance and said, "I'll bet you know Jesus, don't you?" At that her already-happy face broke into uncontainable joy.

"Is it that obvious?" she asked.

When I told her that yes, it was, she seemed extraordinarily delighted. At that moment I understood the Scripture that said, "The joy of the LORD is your strength" (Nehemiah 8:10).

To simply think of Christ produces such joy in most of us, for his name suggests all the wonderful paths our common pilgrimage has traversed. From the moment he saved us, those moments of discord were washed with his sufficiency. At such moments, this psalm makes us understand that Jesus and a sour spirit rarely live long together in our lives,

"For his anger lasts only a moment, but his favor lasts a lifetime; weeping may remain for a night, but rejoicing comes in the morning" (Psalm 30:5).

Questions for Personal Reflection

1. Do you feel joyous when you think about Christ and all he has done for you?

2. Do you carry your joy with you wherever you go?

Day 4: My Service to Others
Read Isaiah 42:1, 10–13

Some years ago a popular cola manufacturer had for its worldwide adver-tising campaign a commercial centering on the wild international elation and global harmony people felt from drinking "soda pop." To be sure, it is a stretch to think the entire world would lay down their separate con-stitutions and ethnic biases and all become one simply from drinking the same cola.

Nonetheless, I think it is exactly the picture that often created in the book of Isaiah the prophet. Here in this passage, the entire world— mountains, deserts, forests, and seas— are caught up in a great and over-whelming song of praise. What the cola manufacturer only dreamed that cola could do, a world of people praising God actually accomplished.

Several years ago I preached in a Hawaiian congregation and was amazed to find that there was no dominant nationality. It was truly an international worship service. For one brief shining moment, I actu-ally felt the Isaiah passage come to life. All nations, it seemed to me, had joined together in that wonderful oneness that only our praise can achieve. Jesus himself has taught the world to sing in perfect harmony. In a world torn by racial prejudice and civil injustice, this message of harmony is most welcome.

Questions for Personal Reflection

1. What can you do to be a part of helping the world to praise God?

2. Do you believe the world can live in harmony?

Day 5: My Personal Worship

Read Leviticus 9:22–24

Let us examine the order of the events that led to the people's praise. First, Aaron, the high priest, made an offering for their sins (which for Christians happened when Jesus paid the price for our sins on the cross). Second, they gathered in the place of public assembly (which for Christians is equal to the church). Third, Aaron blessed all the people (which for Christians is Christ's unforsaking presence). Fourth, the glory of the Lord appeared in real fire that devoured the sacrifice (which for Christians is the guaranteed living presence of the Holy Spirit in our lives whenever we meet). Finally, all the people fell on their faces in praise and worshiped God with their whole hearts.

What was the total effect of this collective adoration? Unity. Worship not only brings God to the people, it also brings the people into oneness. In worship we truly are united in a oneness that makes us into one body functioning as a single organism of praise.

Joy is the great eraser of troublesome individual viewpoints. Take the Promise Keeper movement, for example. Two things mark this movement. Number one: they praise God when they get together. The overwhelming and genuine euphoria of thousands of men praising God cannot help but wash the fatigued spirits of America's men with cleansing and joy.

Number two: when these men praise God, the denominational lines that separate them meet a great spiritual eraser. Differences they thought were significant are scrubbed out by the joy of their focus on Jesus.

Is not this our great hunger of heart as believers? We sing "Draw Me Nearer" as an expression of our hearts, for we are tired of our separateness. We long to be one with Jesus, and when we enter into praise, a wonderful phenomenon begins to happen. Gradually the hard, fast lines that have separated us from God begin to disappear, and like the ancient Israelites we fall face down before him. He unites with us, and enfolded in his glory, we know the great value of human existence.

Questions for Personal Reflection

1. Do you praise God when you are with your friends?

2. How can you personally unite and cause separated people to come together and praise God?

Day 6: David—Joy in the Psalmist's Heart
Read Psalm 23

Whenever we think of David, we see in our minds a man as diverse as the world itself. He was a giant-killer, king, adulterer, and warrior. He was capable of honor, but also capable of crime. He sang to God's glory and embarrassed God's holiness. But his highest office was an office of joy. He was a singer of songs, and those songs, far more than his weaknesses, we hold in our hearts. David sang in joy. David praised God!

He praised God for his providence and care: "The LORD is my shepherd" (Psalm 23:1).

He praised God for his protection: "But you are a shield around me, O LORD" (Psalm 3:3).

He praised God for his brilliant display through all of nature: "The heavens declare the glory of God" (Psalm 19:1).

He praised God when he was insecure: "Trust in the LORD and do good" (Psalm 37:3).

He praised God when he was in trouble:

> *I waited patiently for the LORD;*
> *he turned to me and heard my cry.*
> *He lifted me out of the slimy pit,*
> *out of the mud and mire.*
> —Psalm 40:1–2

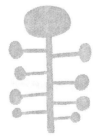

He praised God when he felt the rebuke of his own sin:

> *Have mercy on me, O God,*
> *according to your unfailing love;*
> *according to your great compassion*
> *blot out my transgressions.*
> —Psalm 51:1

Ironically, David gave God joy when he was in need of joy. "Restore to me the joy of your salvation and grant me a willing spirit, to sustain me" (Psalm 51:12).

David was a man of joy, and nothing awakens the soul's liberty like praise. Joy is that rare force in the human heart that creates in us a lightness of being. It places us in a wonderful spirit of triumph. It is the antidote to all despair. It abandons our questioning of the mysteries of his power. Through joy we gain a nearness to God that makes life worthwhile. Those who cannot praise become so sullied by the grime of living that they cannot see God. David sang and was free. His joy is our liberation every time we pick up the Psalms.

The Psalms sing us into a conviction of our own worth. The Psalms lift our heavy souls and restore our amputated wings, and we fly. And soaring over all our sin and trials, we can see all things in perspective and know the size of our troubles is not as large as we suppose.

Only after joy can we see that God is smiling on our need with abundance that only praise makes visible.

Questions for Personal Reflection

1. Do you praise God whether things in your life are good or bad?

2. Did you know you give God joy when you ask to supply joy in your life?

Day 7: Group Discussion

The following questions should take about forty-five minutes to answer and discuss. Each member should answer the first question, leaving the remaining questions open-ended. Everyone need not answer, but be sure all members participate.

1.   *Would you describe yourself as more of an optimist or a pessimist?*

2.   *Why is a positive attitude godly?*

3.   *How do you control your emotions? Tell us about a time when you let your emotions control you.*

4.   *Give an example of how Jesus has brought joy into your life.*

5. Nehemiah 8:10 says, "The joy of the LORD is your strength." Does it make you feel stronger when you rejoice in your love for God? Are there times you feel weak? What could you do to find joy and strength in those times?

6. Based on this week's lesson, list one personal goal you have for the coming week.

Week 3: Joy—Infallible Proof of the Presence of God

Memory Passage for the Week: Zephaniah 3:17

Day 1: Joy—Infallible Proof of the Presence of God

It is impossible to witness the salvation of God and not experience joy. Exodus 15:19–21.

Day 2: The Purpose of God in My Life

Before we were born, the plan for our lives already existed. The scope of God's confidence in us is thrilling. Jeremiah 1:4–5.

Day 3: My Relationship with Christ

God wants us to see that we are chosen, and, best of all, we belong to him. We are to declare our joy—our praises for him who saved us and called us into service. Habakkuk 3:17–18.

Day 4: My Service to Others

Joy is not just something we give to God to keep him happy with our positive attitude. Joy is how we minister to others. 1 Peter 2:9.

Day 5: My Personal Worship

We should praise God with such force of soul that we are transformed by the force. Psalm 150:1–5.

Day 6: A Character Study on Mary of Bethany

Mark 14:1–8

Day 7: Group Discussion

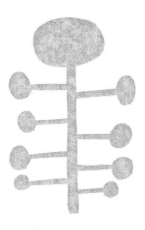

Day 1: Joy—Infallible Proof of the Presence of God
Read Exodus 15:19–21

It is impossible to witness the salvation of God and not experience joy. The Israelites were an unarmed and defenseless horde of slaves. They could neither raise any arms nor produce an effective battle strategy against Pharaoh's mighty infantry. They would have been lost if God had not fought for them.

Then came the miracle of God. A strong east wind held back the waters of the Red Sea, and Israel passed through it on dry ground. The Red Sea had just eradicated all of Israel's enemies. The entire army of Pharaoh was destroyed, and Israel was saved. Miriam, caught up in the rapture of victory, began to praise the God who defends the defenseless. She sang:

> *Sing to the* LORD,
> *for he is highly exalted.*
> *The horse and its rider*
> *he has hurled into the sea.*
> —Exodus 15:21

If this seems less exalted to you than "Amazing Grace," be assured it is the very same theme, and the joy it inspired was also the same.

Joy erupts from all who observe the victories of God. When John Newton saw all that God did in his life, he sang, "Amazing grace, how sweet the sound that saved a wretch like me / I once was lost but now am found; was blind but now I see." When Miriam of Israel saw the victory of God, she, too, sang, of God's amazing grace: "He is highly exalted. The horse and its rider he has hurled into the sea."

Joy is the unhideable, unquenchable, unchangeable, unthinkable, outrageous response of the grateful saved. Miriam was among them. So are you. Rejoice!

Questions for Personal Reflection

1. Do you know people who need saving grace?

2. How will you let them know that God can save them and bring them joy?

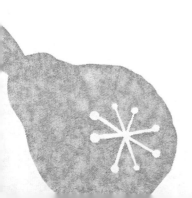

Day 2: The Purpose of God in My Life
Read Jeremiah 1:4–5

Having a calling is the single greatest, lasting impetus to seeing meaning in our lives. So often we hear frustrated people sighing, "What am I here for?" "Why am I in the world?"

Almost any suicide note reeks with a perceived lack of significance and purpose. Some years ago the body of a young girl was pulled out of the Missouri River only blocks from the small apartment where my wife and I lived. Pinned to her seedy, muddy blouse was a note in running faded ink: "I haven't a friend in the world; nobody cares for me." How untrue. God not only cared for her, he had a plan for her life.

We should not try to follow Christ with no explicit sense of purpose. Our own spiritual security can have no real meaning unless we see what Christ wants us to do with his marvelous gift of eternal life. For Jeremiah the purposes of God for his life were rooted in the ages before he was born. He felt dwarfed by all God had called him to do, but he never doubted why he was in the world.

If you are still young in Christ, a full knowledge of his call and all he is going to use you to accomplish would frighten you. But day by day the knowledge that you are in the world for a purpose, and that purpose has made you a business partner with God, will fill you with joy as you begin to see yourself as a creature of ultimate significance.

Questions for Personal Reflection

1. Do you wonder why you are here and what is your purpose in life?

2. Do you feel overwhelmed knowing how much God believes in you?

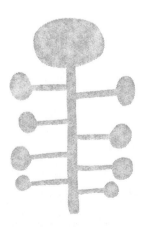

Day 3: My Relationship with Christ

Read Habakkuk 3:17–18

Hard times come. But these times are the classrooms in the school of life. Don't show us a congregation of rich Christians yawning their way through hymns if you want us to believe. Show us poor Christians who never seem to notice their poverty since they've been made rich by a holy God.

Look at what joy teaches others when poor Christians turn to Christ as he enriches them. Christ is their sole sufficiency. The poor Christians are the truly rich Christians.

They praise God when there are no grapes on the vines.

They praise God when the field holds no harvest.

They praise God when there are no sheep in the pen.

They praise God when there are no cattle in the stalls.

We crave such joy, for it never sees God in terms of the stock market or the annuity plan.

God is God—he is enough.

How odd that in the West most fathers seem to want to show their sons how to succeed—how to get on in the world. But good Christian fathers need to show their children how to sing in times of failure as well. We have so few lessons on that.

Joy is not dependent on the sumptuousness of our circumstances but the richness of Christ, who orders all our lives.

Questions for Personal Reflection

1. How often do you praise God?

2. Why do you praise God?

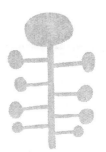

Day 4: My Service to Others
Read 1 Peter 2:9

We are indeed a royal priesthood. And what is it that priests do? They are mediators. They inform the world what God expects and help the world get better acquainted with God.

But notice the kind of priests Peter says we have become: praising priests. We are called to wake the world to wonder—for we have been called out of darkness into his wonderful light.

Praising priests! Jesus wants us to keep the world aware of the virtues of praise. Praise lifts us. It wraps our mundane problems in song. It transports us from a sad-sack mentality to "The Hallelujah Chorus."

Does it really heal us to this extent?

Have you never gotten up on a given Sunday morning, beaten up by life, and told yourself you just didn't feel like going to church? Do not be deceived by your low mood. This is when you need to go. Crawl on in, low as a reptile in your joyless world. Then wait for the praise to begin. It comes. It forces your chin up. It lifts your face toward the colored glass. Soon your heart rebukes you. What's this? You're clapping? Now you're dancing? Praise has done it all. We are the choir leaders of the kingdom. We are the healers of the gloom-chained. We are the priests of praise!

Once the praising has begun, the world itself is mystified by the roar and power of it all. Why? Because praise transforms all it touches. It transforms the "praiser" first, and bit by bit it changes the entire world who stops to hear it. In fact, when time has run its course, praise itself will lure the New Jerusalem from the skies and then keep on singing until the New Jerusalem has replaced the old.

Questions for Personal Reflection

1. Have you ever felt miserable and noticed the change as soon as you praised God?

2. How else do you try and adjust your attitude?

Day 5: My Personal Worship

Read Psalm 150:1–5

One cannot read Psalm 150 without seeing that the joy of our personal worship must be guided by four powerful questions:

- **Where** are we to praise God?
- **Why** are we to praise God?
- **How** are we to praise God?
- **Who** is to praise God?

Where are we to praise God? The psalmist says we should praise God in his sanctuary and in the heavens. Do not be too amazed at this requirement to praise God in the heavens. The heavens themselves represent the transport of great adoration. When we praise, like Paul, we are caught up in such lightness of being that we belong more to the heavens than to our dull and plodding earth.

Why are we to praise God? For all his wonderful works. He has done so much in our lives; we would sin if we kept such wonderful works to ourselves.

How are we to praise God? With all sorts of instruments. Let none claim that accordions, or tambourines, or guitars lack dignity. God must be praised. Our praise should be done neither quietly nor hesitantly. We should praise him with such force of soul that we are transformed by the force.

Who is to praise God? Anyone with a heart and a pulse. Any world is shoddy indeed that will not sing his glory.

Questions for Personal Reflection

1. When do you praise God?

2. Do you help others to praise God?

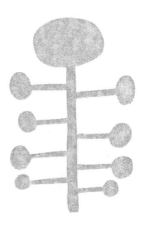

Day 6: Mary of Bethany—Exhibiting Elation
Read Mark 14:1–8

Mary of Bethany is the woman who broke the vial of perfume and poured this costly perfume on Jesus. (We know it is her from comparing this account with the one in John 12.) Not only did she anoint his feet with the nard, but afterward she dried his feet with her hair. One can only imagine the state of heart that drove her to such exhibitionism. She was obviously a woman deeply in love with Christ.

Joy is hopelessly exhibitionistic. It doesn't mean to be so. Joy is no emotion to keep in a bottle and release with propriety in our more controlled moments. Mary of Bethany had to let go of propriety. Jesus was at hand. Extravagance owned the day! One cannot avoid being flamboyant when near the flame of love. Didn't Miriam dance and play the tambourines after the Red Sea crossing? Would you have rebuked Miriam and told her to instead read from the pulpit? When they brought the ark into Jerusalem, David danced before the Lord with all his might. Would you have preferred that David merely walk properly into the city asking for those around him to remain at silent prayer? If so, then you misunderstand the nature of joy. Watch separated lovers reuniting in a railway station. You may suggest that public embracing is not proper, but when these lovers are so full of joy, it is unlikely they will heed your counsel. When joy visits us in full force, and we feel the elation at its zenith, we will praise with elation.

Mary was a woman in love with Jesus. She broke the vial, and the whole house filled with the aroma. Her joy is a call to us. How wonderful it is when the mood of worship is unbridled joy. This is the feeling of those old-fashioned revivals where God was so much adored that the audience abandoned its sense of propriety in favor of exhilarating praise. When the mood came upon them, Jesus was adored. It was, in its own special way, an anointing. It was a fragrance of sweet love, given freely and openly. Do you object that people ought to stay more in control when they praise God? Read this passage again. When praise is directed toward Jesus with him as its sole object, it cares less about what anyone else might think. Joy creates its own right to be. It cares about authenticity, not propriety.

Mary's joy was her anointing. It would become her memorial for ages to come. Call her lacking in propriety, and those who mind their manners will agree. But you will convince no one if you insist that she is a dour soul with little joy. History still smells the sweetness of her perfume. Its aroma freshens the air of the centuries.

Questions for Personal Reflection

1. Do you ever try to control your joy for fear of offending someone?

2. What would you do if someone wanted to control your joy in the Lord?

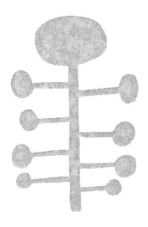

Day 7: Group Discussion

The following questions should take about forty-five minutes to answer and talk about. Each member should answer the first question, and the remaining questions should be open-ended. Everyone need not answer, but be sure all members participate in the discussion these questions create.

1. *What in your life brings you the most joy?*

2. *Miriam sang of God's amazing grace when he parted the Red Sea for the Israelites. Tell about a time in your life when God saved you.*

3. *Why do you believe God has a plan for your life? Tell about a time when you felt called by God to do something specific or to make a change.*

4. *What makes it difficult to praise God when things are going wrong?*

5.   On a scale of 1 to 10, rate the amount of joy you currently experience.

6.   How do you share the joy of God's love with others? Who is someone you know who could use some joy?

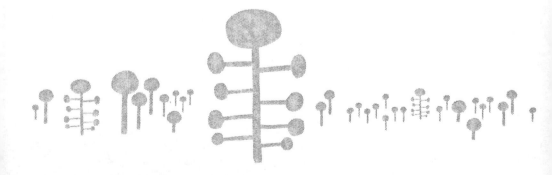

Week 4: Joy—The Reward of Endurance

Memory Passage for the Week: Psalm 126:5–6

Day 1: Joy—The Reward of Endurance

The courage to adhere to God's will for our lives inevitably results in joy.
Esther 8:15–17.

Day 2: God's Purpose in My Life

When we face trials, God enables us with power beyond ourselves to
endure, and to triumph with joy. Acts 16:22–26.

Day 3: My Relationship with Christ

The knowledge of salvation in Christ leads to songs of joy, even in the
face of our struggles. Revelation 7:13–17.

Day 4: My Service to Others

We can rejoice in the knowledge that God hears our prayers and knows all
our troubles. Everyone should know of the comfort and joy God offers us
if we turn to him. Lamentation 3:55–57.

Day 5: My Personal Worship

We can learn from Job, who, in the midst of suffering, found that when he
worshiped, he could bear anything. Job 19:23–27.

Day 6: A Character Study on Philip

Acts 8:8

Day 7: Group Discussion

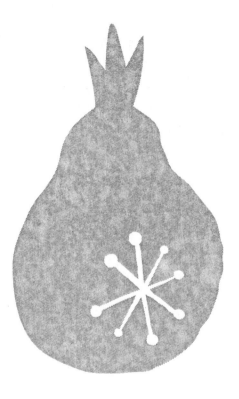

Day 1: Joy—The Reward of Endurance
Read Esther 8:15–17

The great celebration that took place in the book of Esther followed on the heels of Esther's courage. In chapter 4, Esther approached her cousin and adoptive father, Mordecai, and said, "I will go to the king, even though it is against the law. And if I perish, I perish" (v. 16).

Courage often precedes joy. Esther's courage not only saved the Jewish people but led to the institution of the Jewish Festival of Lights. Esther acted in a spirit of courage because she knew that what she was about to do was right. The personal cost to her was not as great a concern to her as was her obedience to principle. Esther rose high among Old Testament heroes for one simple reason: she was not for sale. Her convictions were in line with her heart in heaven. Her life was up for negotiation but her beliefs were not.

She was a woman who dared to stand up for truth in a pro-masculine world. To face power structures with faith in God is all-important. To lobby for truth is to face power with integrity. I wrote a small quatrain in one of my novels years ago:

> *The original sin is the ultimate sin—*
> *Claim thrones and be gods as you may!*
> *And the last pair alive, like the first pair alive,*
> *Would rather have power than obey!*

I have long admired the martyrs and all those who very clearly say: "I believe what I believe, I preach Christ, because Christ is all that matters." Esther is the matron model of all who cherish truth: "I go into the king which is not according to custom and if I perish, I perish." Compromise was out of the question.

Questions for Personal Reflection

1. Does your life reflect what you believe?

2. Have you ever been afraid to share your faith?

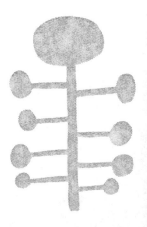

Day 2: God's Purpose in My Life

Read Acts 16:22–26

Tears have a way of sifting and refining our praise. Singing through our tears is the best music. Paul and Silas sang in jail. They were there as a result of their honoring God's purpose in their lives. Their praise was that honest joy earned by standing true when it is most difficult.

Joy is one of the most frequent rewards of endurance. Singing and trials go together better than people might think, especially once the trial is over. So it is with Paul and Silas. There is a fourfold step in moving between trial and joy. First, we face the trial. Second, God enables us with power beyond ourselves. Third, we trust and win—or at least survive. And finally, we sing.

Joy is the end result of facing Satan and triumphing over him. Remember the disciples in Luke 10:17? They returned from their preaching and healing tour in great joy. "Lord," they exulted, "even the demons submit to us in your name!" One wonders if they were not close to song as the joy of their triumph swept over them.

Martin Luther felt the same elation of triumph over Satan when he wrote:

> *And though this world with devils filled,*
> *should threaten to undo us,*
> *We will not fear for God has willed*

his truth to triumph through us:
The Prince of Darkness grim,
We tremble not for him;
His rage we can endure,
For, lo, his doom is sure,
One little word shall fell him.
—"A Mighty Fortress"

Luther's steadfastness illustrates the point: endurance and triumph produce joy.

Questions for Personal Reflection

1. Do you feel there are things you cannot do without God?

2. Do you ever feel God holding you up during times of trouble?

Day 3: My Relationship with Christ
Read Revelation 7:13–17

Joy is the mood of heaven. These who sing in Revelation 7 came out of great trials. Their robes were made white having been dipped in the blood of the Lamb. Their song is recorded in Revelation 7:10. It is a simple song: "Salvation belongs to our God, who sits on the throne." Probably it was the very kind of song martyrs sang during their martyrdoms. The martyrs must have sung to combat the pain they felt. They must have sung, and their singing surely pleased God even as it baffled their persecutors.

It was customary during the Middle Ages to blind canaries by sticking hot needles in their tiny eyes. The cruelty done to these tiny creatures left them in a darkness that knew no way to endure their dumb existence but to sing. So the birds sang, night was all they knew forever, and the only punctuation for their unending night was the melody that they themselves created.

The martyrs in Revelation 7, too, knew only a dark world. Yet in the darkness they endured and remained faithful. They died singing because often it is the only response that makes earth tolerable.

Could it be that joy is the only sensible response that we can make when we hurt and find no light in our endless nights of hope? Singing may be the best response hurting Christians can make to a senseless world.

Questions for Personal Reflection

1. Do you sing when you hurt? Do you pray?

2. Do you praise God no matter how hard things seem?

Day 4: My Service to Others
Read Lamentations 3:55—57

Let us examine this brief excerpt from Jeremiah's weeping lamentations. Phrase by phrase, here is how our endurance may be resolved at last in joy:

I called on your name, O Lord ... (Lamentations 3:55).

This is the wise thing to do in times of unbearable hurt.

There is no other name that saves.

From the depths of the pit ... (v. 55).

Despair is a megaphone in the hand of prayer. It amplifies all that we feel and makes it audible in the courts of heaven.

You heard my plea ... (v. 56).

What the weeping heart whispers is heard by heaven as a shout.

Do not close your ears to my cry for relief ... (v. 56).

God does not close his ears to our cries. He keeps his ear trained to hear the sobbing of his children. He hears their laughter, and he smiles. He hears their petitions and is thoughtful. But when he hears their sobbing, God orders the angels into quiet, so that all of heaven may listen and care.

You came near when I called you ... (v. 57).

One call to our heavenly Father and the remoteness is over. Heaven gives up its cosmic address; the throne of God becomes an armchair of warm rapport; and God—who once seemed starry galaxies away—now lives on our block.

And you said, "Do not fear!" (v. 57).

God is saying, "I have seen your problems, and from my perspective, your problems are not too large for me."

So, it is time for joy, says God, and your lamentations are no longer appropriate. We are not to keep this joy to ourselves, but to share the good news of the comfort and assurance we have in the God who knows all our troubles and hears every prayer.

Questions for Personal Reflection

1. How do you keep a positive attitude when times are tough?

2. Do you ask God to help you spread joy to others when they are hurting?

Day 5: My Personal Worship
Read Job 19:23–27

It is, perhaps, not possible to read these verses without feeling Job's attempt to break through the silence of God. Job felt that he was not heard by heaven. He was enduring his hardships all alone and thought God didn't seem to care. He cried out:

> *Though I cry, "I've been wronged!" I get no response;*
> *though I call for help, there is no justice.*
> *He has blocked my way so I cannot pass;*
> *he has shrouded my paths in darkness.*
> *He has stripped me of my honor*
> *and removed the crown from my head.*
> *He tears me down on every side till I am gone;*
> *he uproots my hope like a tree.*
> —Job 19:7–10

Job honestly felt that no one should ever have to meet the silence of God—particularly when he was so needy—and have his despair go unnoticed. Surely no one should ever have to die with his suffrage unrecorded. He suffered much, and it seemed to him that God didn't care. Thus he cried, "Oh, that my words were recorded, that they were written on a scroll, that they were inscribed with an iron tool on lead, or engraved in rock forever!" (vv. 23–24).

Still, following deep pain, hope finds enough joy to sing. After despair there was a kind of instant joy when Job cried and knew that God still inhabited his silences. Then he knew that his Redeemer lived and would stand upon the earth one day.

Questions for Personal Reflection

1. Do you keep praying and praising God even if you don't hear an answer?

2. Do you feel that with God you are never really alone and he will enable you to withstand anything?

Day 6: Philip—The Joy of Revival
Read Acts 8:8

Acts chapter 8 divides Philip's life into three major incidents of joy. In the first incident he preached in Samaria (vv. 1–8). When the revival was over, great preaching and miracles and exorcism had occurred. The cumulative effect of the meeting was that God was doing business in the lives of a great many people. It was the single comment of Philip in Samaria that there was "great joy in that city" (v. 8). Great joy is the mark of revival.

In the second visitation of joy, Philip confronted Simon Magus (vv. 9–15). The people of Samaria called Simon Magus a stupendous illusionist, a great power. They were spellbound by this magician. Peter and John visited the Samaritan revival and were amazed at the power of all things done in the name of the Spirit. When the apostles laid their hand on the new converts, the power of God fell on them, and again the joy was spectacular. It was then that Simon Magus encountered the great power of the Holy Spirit.

Seeing this done, Simon also wanted the Holy Spirit's power. But Peter said to him, "May your money perish with you, because you thought you could buy the gift of God with money! You have no part or share in this ministry, because your heart is not right before God" (vv. 20–23).

We are not told that joy accompanied this particular confrontation, but it must have been so, for this baptism of God, this wonderful spiritual outpouring, spilled out through the villages and towns of Samaria.

The third outpouring of Philip's joyous kingdom revival occurred when he met an Ethiopian eunuch and convinced him to join the kingdom of God. He baptized the eunuch, and then the Spirit of the Lord whisked Philip away, and the eunuch was by himself. But the joy went on and on. When the eunuch left the waters of baptism, he, too, was filled with elation and went on his way rejoicing (v. 39).

Philip, in Acts 8, remains a study in the joy that results from revival. How good it would be to experience that joy throughout our own land. But we must remember that Philip didn't get the joy because he wanted the joy. The joy came because he wanted to please Christ. When revival renews people's lives with a desire for godly obedience, joy always comes.

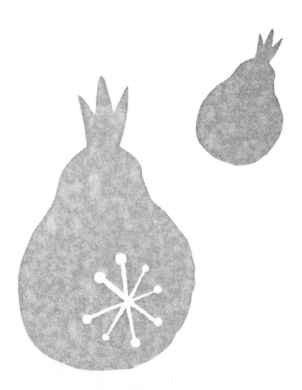

Questions for Personal Reflection

1. Have you experienced spontaneous outbursts of praise and joy in God's name?

2. Have you witnessed the revival and outpouring of joy when God comes into joyless lives?

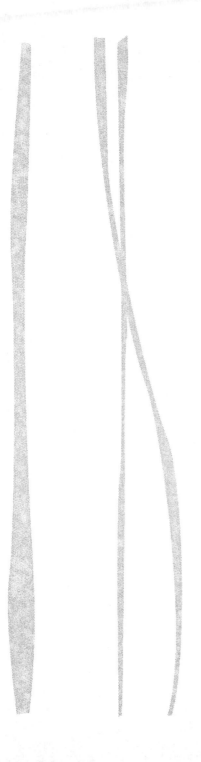

Day 7: Group Discussion

The following questions should take about forty-five minutes to answer and discuss. Each member should answer the first question, leaving the remaining questions open-ended. Everyone need not answer, but be sure all members participate.

1.   *What in your life requires the most endurance?*

2.   *Can you relate to the statement "endurance and triumph produce joy"? In what way(s)?*

3. *Tell us about a time when you experienced significant joy even in the midst of a terrible situation?*

4. *When has God's power seemed very visible to you?*

5. Do you experience joy in special circumstances or in times of praise, but have a hard time keeping that joy going and carrying it through your days? Explain.

6. What are some ways to keep one another joyful in the midst of our busy lives?

Week 5: Joy—Focusing on a Higher Reality

Memory Passage for the Week: Psalm 32:11

Day 1: Joy—Focusing on a Higher Reality

Joy is the automatic result of seeing God in action, of focusing on a higher reality. 1 Kings 18:20–21, 38–39.

Day 2: The Purpose of God in My Life

Joy comes to us in all kinds of ways—in ways as different as God's purposes for each of us. Ezekiel 1:4–8, 25–28.

Day 3: My Relationship with Christ

Joy causes us to deepen our adoration as we fall increasingly more in love with Christ. Revelation 1:12–16.

Day 4: My Service to Others

During Phillip's revival among the Samaritans, joy broke out among the people as they began to witness what God was doing among them. Acts 8:4–8.

Day 5: My Personal Worship

Joy and pain are both elements of focus in our worship. Pain creates a need for God, and joy is the footprint of his passage into our lives. 2 Corinthians 12:1–6.

Day 6: The Parable of the Lost Sheep

Luke 15:1–7 (TLB)

Day 7: Group Discussion

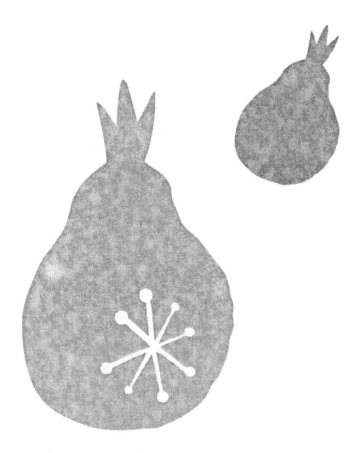

Day 1: Joy—Focusing on a Higher Reality

Read 1 Kings 18:20–21, 38–39

Nothing brings joy to the human heart like actually beholding the power of God in action. Elijah set up on Mount Carmel the arena for just such a display in 1 Kings 18:20–21. He threw out a challenge: "How long will you waver between two opinions? If the LORD is God, follow him; but if Baal is God, follow him" (v. 21). In this dramatic contest between the living God and idolatry, the fire of God fell and the people, in high elation, shouted, "The LORD, he is God! The LORD—he is God!" (v. 39)

Joy is the automatic result of seeing God in action, of focusing on a higher reality. In so many contemporary churches we forget this great truth. We somehow feel that joy is our responsibility. We plan productively and coordinate creatively. We feel that if we can really get the people singing, joy will come: a kind of "Hallelujah hype." Hype and joy can, at times, closely resemble one another, but the heart that is hungry for the visitation of God's power will always know the difference.

When the power comes near, the joy proclaims itself. It's like the electrical phenomenon of felt and silk. When they are close, the static fire can actually be seen. When we focus on the transforming reality of God, joy is the result. It always is and always will be.

Questions for Personal Reflection

1. Have you ever seen God in action, transforming people with joy? Explain.

2. Is it sometimes hard to remember that joy is not your responsibility, that joy comes from God's power? Give an example.

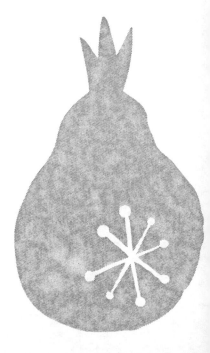

Day 2: The Purpose of God in My Life
Read Ezekiel 1:4–8, 25–28

Ezekiel saw a windstorm, a cloud of flashing lightning, and a sky on fire like glowing metal. He then saw four men with sixteen faces and sixteen wings. Ezekiel saw these four creatures flying after a spirit in the midst of fire, back and forth like lightning flashing erratically in the sky (Ezekiel 1:11–14).

This is the account of a Picasso-type religious experience. Ezekiel didn't see the kingdom of God like everyone else. It came to him in vivid illustrations that proved his Lord was no pastel God—no, this was a God who could put stripes, prints, plaids, and neon colors together in such a way that he settled on the earth in indescribable joy.

But best of all, when this God of the wild palette spoke, there was work to be done, and Ezekiel received his purpose, wrote down his color-filled visions, and went off to do his work. Joy speaks to us in all kinds of ways—in ways as different to each of us as his purposes for each of us.

Questions for Personal Reflection

1. Have you felt the joy of the Lord?

2. How does the Lord speak to you?

Day 3: My Relationship with Christ

Read Revelation 1:12—16

The mood of the book of Revelation is a strong intermingling of joy and apocalyptic portent. The reigning Christ is presented in this tale of futurism and conquering saints. But the songs of joy that arise from it are truly inspiring. Consider the texts from which so many songs that furnish our worship are derived:

> *Holy, Holy, Holy ... Lord God Almighty.*
> —Revelation 4:8

> *Worthy is the Lamb, who was slain,*
> *to receive power and wealth and wisdom and strength*
> *and honor and glory and praise!*
> —Revelation 5:12

> *The kingdom of the world has become*
> *the kingdom of our Lord and of his Christ,*
> *and he will reign for ever and ever.*
> —Revelation 11:15

> *Hallelujah! For our Lord God almighty reigns.*
> —Revelation 19:6

The great book of Revelation focuses on the joy that comes from a rich encounter with God. Revelation was written by a fisherman whom Christ called into service years earlier. This proves that even a fisherman may come up with glory when he has seen the heavens open, and his praise is furnished by a face-to-face encounter with Christ.

Questions for Personal Reflection

1. What will you say when you encounter Jesus face to face?

2. Do you know anyone whose life has changed dramatically because of knowing God?

Day 4: My Service to Others
Read Acts 8:4—8

The eight-word epigram penned by Luke to describe the Samaritan revival was, "So there was great joy in that city" (Acts 8:8).

There were miracles, exorcisms, sermons, and signs. God's power is a
simple recipe for waking the world to joy around us. These are the kinds
of things that can happen when we begin to serve others. Yet this higher
reality that brings such joy hides in simple things that are near at hand.
Martin Luther felt the higher reality lived in much lower verities:

> *If we had eyes and ears we would be able to see and hear*
> *what the wheat says to us, "Rejoice in God, eat and drink,*
> *use me to serve your neighbors. Soon I will fill the barns." If I*
> *were not deaf, I would hear the cows say: "Be glad, we bring*
> *you butter and cheese. Eat and drink and give to others." So*
> *the hens say, "We lay eggs for you." And the birds, "Be joy-*
> *ful, we are hatching chicks." ... So speak all the animals to*
> *us, and everyone should say, "I will use what God has given*
> *me and I will give to others."*
>
> *But as Christ affected this cure He sighed because He*
> *knew that as soon as man's tongue was restored he would*
> *misuse it.*[2]

Joy is easy to come by. We just have to open our eyes and ears, and God's provisions will overwhelm us. It will never be more authentic than after we have served someone else and given all the credit to Christ.

Questions for Personal Reflection

1. How does your church serve others?

2. What good things have happened in your church because it serves others?

Day 5: My Personal Worship

Read 2 Corinthians 12:1–6

Paul speaks here of his religious experience. He saw Christ! He saw him like Isaiah did, "high and exalted" (Isaiah 6:1). Paul found the exact form of the religious experience hard to describe later. "Whether it was in or out of the body," Paul wasn't sure (2 Corinthians 12:2). Perhaps that is the danger of religious experience. We may experience great feelings of religious transport, but we later are at a loss to tell the exact nature of the experience.

But worship is religious experience. How poor we would be without it. What are those things that happened to Paul in the transporting experience that we want to characterize our own walk with Christ?

1. He was "caught up" (v. 2). We should feel that same sense of transport, a lifting of our lives above the commonplace and the mundane.

2. "In the body or out" ... Paul didn't know (vv. 2–3). We ought to understand that if we have a vital affair with Christ, it will come to us within the context of such overwhelming mystery that we will likely not be able to understand it ourselves, let alone explain it to others. Yet we need that very kind of experience. For a God who we cannot encounter with mys-

teries that are bigger than us would be too much like us to be of any real use.

3. Paul "heard inexpressible things, things that a man is not permitted to tell" (v. 4). This is the delicious case of all our "prayer-closet" experiences. We go deep in Christ, and the intimacy of our relationship is glorious. But intimacy—physical or spiritual—is the language of two and cannot really be communicated to groups. Our personal worship will from time to time provide us with such a warm and transporting camaraderie that we will feel at a loss in our every attempt to define it.

Questions for Personal Reflection

1. Do you feel you have a close, intimate relationship with Christ? Explain.

2. What can you do to deepen your relationship with the Lord?

Day 6: The Parable of the Lost Sheep

LUKE 15:1–7 (TLB)

Dishonest tax collectors and other notorious sinners often came to listen to Jesus'
sermons; but this caused complaints from the Jewish religious leaders and the
experts on Jewish law because he was associating with such despicable people—
even eating with them! So Jesus used this illustration:

"If you had a hundred sheep and one of them strayed away and
was lost in the wilderness, wouldn't you leave the ninety-nine others to go and search for the lost one until you found it? And then
you would joyfully carry it home on your shoulders. When you ar-
rived you would call together your friends and neighbors to rejoice
with you because your lost sheep was found. Well, in the same way
heaven will be happier over one lost sinner who returns to God
than over ninety-nine others who haven't strayed away!"

Questions for Personal Reflection

1. Has there ever been a time in your life when you strayed from God? What happened?

2. Have you ever experienced the joy of being "found" by God? What was that experience like?

Day 7: Group Discussion

The following questions should take about forty-five minutes to answer and discuss. Each member should answer the first question, leaving the remaining questions open-ended. Everyone need not answer, but be sure all members participate.

1. *Which of this week's daily lessons stood out to you the most? Why?*

2. *What is the difference between hype and joy? Have you ever witnessed praise that was hype instead of true joy? If yes, explain.*

3. *Tell us about a time when you experienced a miracle.*

4.   When have you felt overwhelmed by joy?

5.   Joy, like the rest of the fruits of the Spirit, is a gift given to us by the Holy Spirit. How have you seen the Holy Spirit at work this past week?

6.   Do you know any lost sheep? What can you do to bring them to the Lord?

Week 6: Joy—The Reveling of Angels

Memory Passage for the Week: Psalm 148:1–2

Day 1: Joy—The Reveling of Angels

Joy is always a result of the lost being found. It always sets the angels singing. Luke 15:1–7.

Day 2: The Purpose of God in My Life

Heaven rejoices every time we stand firm in a trial of any kind. Matthew 4:10–11.

Day 3: My Relationship with Christ

When Jesus was born, the world was blessed, and salvation for humankind was on the way. What else would any God-fearing angel do but sing? Luke 2:13–14.

Day 4: My Service to Others

Hospitality: Why is God so interested in it? Guests can be souls who bring something unexpected to our lives. They could be angels, and we might not be aware of it at the time. Hebrews 13:2.

Day 5: My Personal Worship

Angels command us to praise. Joy is their business. To praise God, even for a moment, tells us why we are in the world. Psalm 103:20–21.

Day 6: Verses for Further Reflection

Day 7: Group Discussion

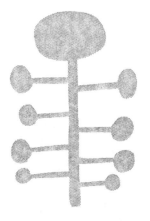
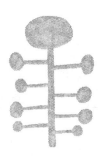

Day 1: Joy—The Reveling of Angels
Read Luke 15:1–7

In Luke 15, joy was sponsored by the recovering of things that were lost: a lost sheep (vv. 1–7), a lost coin (vv. 8–10), and a lost boy (vv. 11–31). Jesus remarked in the first two cases (and it was certainly implied in the last case) that it was the retrieval of the lost that set the angels singing.

Across the years I have seen many found who were once spiritually lost. Their coming to grace always initiated a revival; often a whole family would be converted. This happened person by person as the various relatives—influenced by the uncontainable joy of those who had found Christ—would themselves come to Christ.

I recall one woman whom one of our younger members led to Christ. Within a week or two I led her husband to Christ. Shortly after her husband found Christ, he asked me if I would present Christ to his son, a city attorney. The young lawyer accepted Christ, and on the Sunday when the young man came forward to confess his faith, his father in an opposite corner of the balcony also came. They were both in tears of utter joy as they met at the altar.

The effect of these two men embracing at the altar with tears of joy was witnessed by the entire church. Joy became so abundant in our congregation that for the next few months, many more came in an extended season of joy to confess Christ. Joy is inevitably a result of the lost being found. It always sets the angels singing as it works that same kind of wonder here on earth.

Questions for Personal Reflection

1. Have you experienced one conversion leading to another?

2. Do you look for the spiritually lost to bring them to Jesus?

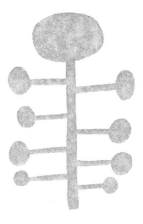

Day 2: The Purpose of God in My Life
Read Matthew 4:10–11

Angels come after we answer our temptations with steadfastness. Joy is a close relative of self-control. Joy is the friend of those who know how to say *no* and who know when to say *no*, and can say *no* clearly so that it doesn't sound like *maybe*.

How the world is missing this single syllable of glory.

The child who wants to stand up for the biblical truth in a classroom needs the courage to say a good, kingdom-blessed *no*.

The executive who is being offered an illegal embezzlement option needs the power of a good, clear *no*.

The preacher who faces the temptation to move to a larger and wealthier parish should be motivated by better adjectives than "larger and wealthier." He needs the courage to say, "*No!*"

The college student who is looking at the false promises of a pill and the coming party needs the power of *no*.

To any or all of these who can say *no*, remember the angels are hovering about waiting for your response. If you can respond as you should, you can be sure that temptations conquered are the soil of joy.

Consider the words of Joshua 1:9: "Have I not commanded you? Be strong and courageous. Do not be terrified; do not be discouraged, for the LORD your God will be with you wherever you go." And when you have stood true, you will also not be alone, for you will be standing in the company of some very proud angels.

Questions for Personal Reflection

1. Do you have the strength to stand up for your beliefs?

2. Can you say "no"? Explain.

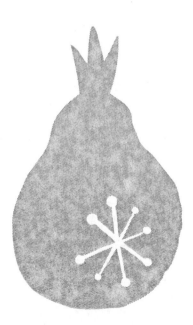

Day 3: My Relationship with Christ
Read Luke 2:13–14

In fictionalizing the Bethlehem angels, I picture how frightening their
joy must be when you meet angels close up. A sky full of exuberance, as
occurred in Luke 2, must have been a paralyzing event. But the shepherds
were, once the fear had passed, ready to be filled with joy. The testimony
of one of the shepherds must have sounded something like this:

> *It was just after midnight when the gold broke all around*
> *us! The light stung my eyes ... I choked and gagged. I don't*
> *know why—I must have been allergic to all that light. I*
> *was terrified. These big, silvery white beings poured out of*
> *the skies, like a tangled flock of big geese ... those bright, big*
> *fellows exploded out of the shattered blackness and fell like the*
> *sparks from the blacksmith's forge all around our feet. My*
> *skin started to crawl. My eyes twitched. The hair on my*
> *neck prickled and then tried to crawl down my collar.*
>
> *Name any fear I've ever felt before this, and I'll deny the*
> *force of it. I never in all my life was afraid till that night. The*
> *angels did it all. They burst upon me, forcing me into sheer*
> *terror of that much splendor at midnight. It was like the dark*
> *nightmares you have as a child, but it was a nightmare made*
> *of light. I saw everything, and I trembled.*

All of a sudden the whole flock—or whatever you call a group of angels—started singing, "Glory to God in the highest and on earth, peace to men of goodwill!"

Then they were gone, just like that! When all that light and noise was over, things got dark and quiet.[3]

Things may be "dark and quiet" once joy settles, but having praised God we are never quite the same again. This is particularly true in the case of our relationship with Christ. Praise him briefly and live for a day. Praise him regularly and live forever.

Questions for Personal Reflection

1. Have you ever been frightened by being so blessed with joy?

2. Do you think you can have too much joy?

Day 4: My Service to Others

Read Hebrews 13:2

There are times when we may entertain angels unaware. Take, for example, Sarai's experience of cooking for a trio of vagabond nomads and suddenly discovering that they had been sent from the Lord:

GENESIS 18:1–2; 6–15

The LORD appeared to Abraham near the great trees of Mamre—while he was sitting at the entrance to his tent in the heat of the day. Abraham looked up the saw three men standing nearby. When he saw them, he hurried from the entrance of his tent to meet them and bowed low to the ground....

So Abraham hurried into the tent to Sarah. "Quick," he said, "get three seahs of fine flour and knead it and bake some bread. Then he ran to the herd and selected a choice, tender calf and gave it to a servant, who hurried to prepare it. He then brought some curds and milk and the calf that had been prepared, and set these before them. While they ate, he stood near them under a tree.

"Where is your wife Sarah?" they asked him.

"There, in the tent," he said.

Then the LORD said, "I will surely return to you about this time next year, and Sarah your wife will have a son."

Now Sarah was listening at the entrance to the tent, which was behind him. Abraham and Sarah were already old and well advanced in years, and Sarah was past the age of childbearing. So Sarah laughed to herself as she thought, "After I am worn out and my master is old, will I now have this pleasure?"

Then the LORD said to Abraham, "Why did Sarah laugh and say, 'Will I really have a child, now that I am old?' Is anything too hard for the LORD? I will return to you at the appointed time next year and Sarah will have a son."

Sarah was afraid, so she lied and said, "I did not laugh."

But he said, "Yes, you did laugh."

Angels are subtle; Sarah laughed at their prophecy and was instructed to name her son "Laughter". It is good to treat vagabonds seriously. Angels are all around, and you never know when you might encounter one.

Questions for Personal Reflection

1. Have you ever met a stranger who made a strong impact on your life? Explain.

2. Do you share laughter and the joy of the Lord with all you meet? Why or why not?

Day 5: My Personal Worship
Read Psalm 103:20–21

Praise the LORD, you his angels (Psalm 103:20).

   Are we not his messengers of joy?

   In this gloomy world do we not need an occasional extra baptism of happiness just to feel life is worth it?

You mighty ones who do his bidding (v. 20).

   His bidding is not grievous,

   His task for us is the reason we exist,

   Therefore whatever work he commands us is joy.

Obey his word (v. 20).

   Obedience will make the mute sing!

   Obedience and music are both divine compositions.

   Those who obey have a reason to sing.

   Those who sing have a reason to obey.

Praise the LORD, all his heavenly hosts (v. 21).

   Notice, God said *all* his heavenly hosts.

   We will have no dour angels here who will not sing.

   Let there not be even one grumpy angel in the presence of God,

   For remember Lucifer may have begun his fall,

By skipping his morning *alleluiabs*.
Praise him all who do his will.
Joy is the business of angels.
Joy is humanity's business too.

Questions for Personal Reflection

1. Do you believe joy is your business? Why or why not?

2. Are you a messenger of joy for the Lord? In what way(s)?

Day 6: Verses for Further Reflection

Luke 15:10: In the same way, I tell you, there is rejoicing in the presence of the angels of God over one sinner who repents.

John 16:20: I tell you the truth, you will weep and mourn while the world rejoices. You will grieve, but your grief will turn to joy.

John 16:22: So with you: Now is your time of grief, but I will see you again and you will rejoice, and no one will take away your joy.

John 16:24: Until now you have not asked for anything in my name. Ask and you will receive, and your joy will be complete.

John 17:13: I am coming to you now, but I say these things while I am still in the world, so that they may have the full measure of my joy within them.

Romans 15:13: May the God of hope fill you with all joy and peace as you trust in him, so that you may overflow with hope by the power of the Holy Spirit.

Philippians 4:4: Rejoice in the Lord always. I will say it again: Rejoice!

ACTS 16:13–34

The mood of this passage is joy! The two incidents of conversion are separated by imprisonment and pain. But wherever people come to faith in Christ, the resulting mood is joy.

On the Sabbath we went outside the city gate to the river, where we expected to find a place of prayer. We sat down and began to speak to the women who had gathered there. One of those listening was a woman named Lydia, a dealer in purple cloth from the city of Thyatira, who was a worshiper of God. The Lord opened her heart to respond to Paul's message. When she and the members of her household were baptized, she invited us to her home. "If you consider me a believer in the Lord," she said, "come and stay at my house." And she persuaded us.

Once when we were going to the place of prayer, we were met by a slave girl who had a spirit by which she predicted the future. She earned a great deal of money for her owners by fortune-telling. This girl followed Paul and the rest of us, shouting, "These men are servants of the Most High God, who are telling you the way to be saved." She kept this up for many days. Finally Paul became so troubled that he turned around and said to the spirit, "In the name of Jesus Christ I command you to come out of her!" At that moment the spirit left her.

When the owners of the slave girl realized that their hope of making money was gone, they seized Paul and Silas and dragged them into the marketplace to face the authorities. They brought them before the magistrates and said, "These men are Jews, and are throwing our city into an uproar by advocating customs unlawful for us Romans to accept or practice."

The crowd joined in the attack against Paul and Silas, and the magistrates ordered them to be stripped and beaten. After they had been severely flogged, they were thrown into prison, and the jailer was commanded to guard them carefully. Upon receiving such orders, he put them in the inner cell and fastened their feet in the stocks.

About midnight Paul and Silas were praying and singing hymns to God, and the other prisoners were listening to them. Suddenly there was such a violent earthquake that the foundations of the prison were shaken. At once all the prison doors flew open, and everybody's chains came loose. The jailer woke up, and when he saw the prison doors open, he drew his sword and was about to kill himself because he thought the prisoners had escaped. But Paul shouted, "Don't harm yourself! We are all here!"

The jailer called for lights, rushed in and fell trembling before Paul and Silas. He then brought them out and asked, "Sirs, what must I do to be saved?"

They replied, "Believe in the Lord Jesus and you will be saved— you and your household." Then they spoke the word of the Lord to him and to all the others in his house. At that hour of the night the jailer took them and washed their wounds; then immediately he and all his family were baptized. The jailer brought them into his house and set a meal before them; he was filled with joy because he had come to believe in God—he and his whole family.

Questions for Personal Reflection

1. What are some ways you can share your joy with your family?

2. What are some ways you can share your joy with the world?

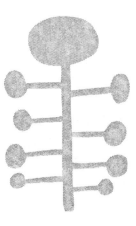

Day 7: Group Discussion

The following questions should take about forty-five minutes to answer and discuss. Each member should answer the first question, leaving the remaining questions open-ended. Everyone need not answer, but be sure all members participate.

1. *What have you lost that is of great value to you?*

2. *What does it mean to be spiritually lost?*

3.   *Do you believe that angels are around us, but that we may be unaware of their presence? Do you think you have ever encountered an angel?*

4.   *When have you felt protected by an angel?*

5. In Acts 16:34–35, the jailer and his entire family were filled with God because they came to believe in God. If you have asked Christ to come into your life, was it was recently, or was it years ago? Do you still experience joy in knowing you are saved?

6. Which of the verses for further reflection is your favorite? What does that verse mean, and why is it significant to you?

ENDNOTES

1. *Calvin Miller,* Star Riders of Ren *(San Francisco, CA: Harper & Row, 1983),* 140.

2, *Martin Luther, from* The Book of Jesus, *edited by Calvin Miller (New York: Simon & Schuster, 1996), 275.*

3. *Calvin Miller,* An Owner's Manual for the Unfinished Soul *(Wheaton, IL: Harold Shaw Publishers, 1997) 157–58,*

PRAYER JOURNAL

Use the following pages to record both prayer requests and answers.

PRAYER JOURNAL